Other QUESTA guides

Walks with Children in the Lake District
Buttermere and the Vale of Lorton
Borrowdale
Ullswater
Around Coniston
Ambleside and Grasmere
South Lakeland
Around Windermere
Around Kendal

Walks with Children in the Yorkshire Dales
Wharfedale
Swaledale and Wensleydale

Short Walks series
Short Walks in the Eden Valley and North Pennines

Walks with Children
in the Lake District

BUTTERMERE
and the
VALE OF LORTON
Ron Bickerton

A QUESTAGuide

ADVICE TO READERS

Readers are advised that while the author had made every effort to ensure the accuracy of this guidebook, changes can occur which may affect the contents. The Publishers would welcome notes of any changes you find.

Maps:
The maps accompanying the walks in this book are purely diagrammatic, and have been based on maps produced by (and with the permission of) Harvey Maps.
© Harvey Maps 1997-2004

Also by Ron Bickerton

Walks with Children in the Lake District
Around Coniston
Keswick and the Newlands Valley

Published by
Questa Publishing Ltd
PO Box 520, Bamber Bridge, Preston,
Lancashire PR5 8LF
and printed by
Carnmor Print, 95/97 London Road, Preston,
Lancashire PR1 4BA

CONTENTS

EXPLANATORY NOTES

Introduction: Questa Walks with Children are intended to introduce young people to hill walking. They range from short, simple river or lakeside ambles, to fairly energetic ascents of fells, sometimes to a considerable height. The walks are not graded, but are intended for groups, with supervised children roughly between the ages of six and fifteen.

Only parents, of course, know just how energetic, determined and resilient their own children are, and so each of the walks gives no more than an indication of the distance to be walked, and the amount of ascent, not necessarily all in one go, you can expect to face. All of the chosen walks have been done with children, and children of all ages have been seen happily plodding along them - they do have remarkable tenacity and boundless energy at times.

But these walks aim to do more than give route descriptions. They aim to educate young and old alike in the interests of the countryside, and the history that surrounds it. So, at the end of each walk a few brief notes tell you what you might find along the way.

Maps: Simple diagrammatic maps accompany each route description. These are based on Harveys Walker's Maps, a specialist map, just for walkers, produced on a waterproof material.

The maps in this book are to scale, either 1:25000 (2½ in to 1 mile~4 cm to 1 km), or 1:40000 (approx. 1½ in to 1 mile~2½ cm to 1 km). These should prove adequate, in good weather conditions, to guide you round the walks, but you are advised always to carry a more detailed and extensive map of the area.

It is recommended that you buy Harveys Walker's Maps if you wish to learn more about the countryside beyond the limited range of our diagrammatic maps. To cover all the walks in this book, you will need two maps: North West Lakeland and Western Lakeland.

Footpaths: Almost all the walks are on public rights of way, permissive paths, or routes which have been used over a period of many years by custom and practice, but any mention of a path does not imply that a right of way exists.

It is unlikely, however, that you will be prevented from following any of the walks mentioned in this book, but you are asked to stick to the paths at all times, especially where they are waymarked, or go through or near farmyards, to be sensitive to the work of the hill farmers, particularly at lambing time, and to keep any dogs you may have with you, under strict and close control at all times.

Equipment: It is important to go well-equipped into the fells, and for everyone this means adequate footwear and waterproof clothing. Small and growing feet will benefit all the more if footwear more substantial than wellington boots or trainers are worn, and will reduce the risk of slipping.

There are rough and wet patches on most of the walks, and for these you will find that modern walking boots with a cleated rubber sole are the best footwear. This remains true even during dry spells in summer: trainers, for example, offer no support to ankles, and while they might be adequate for walking along streets, they cannot cope with steep grassy slopes.

The Lake District, alas, is frequently wet, and a good waterproof should always be carried, along with an extra pullover, cardigan or jacket to compensate for the lower temperatures you will experience as you climb higher, or walk close by the lakes.

Warm trousers, not jeans (which are useless when wet, and offer no protection), are advised, though you don't need expensive walking breeches.

Carry extra food and drink, along with your waterproofs and spare clothing, in a small rucsac.

You must always carry a compass, and understand how to use it properly. If you wish to learn more about the skills needed for walking in the hills, you might consider *The Hillwalker's Manual*, by Bill Birkett (Cicerone Press).

Finally, remember to take with you the good sense to turn back if the weather suddenly changes for the worst.

Route Directions: All the walks start from a car park or convenient parking place, but do remember to secure your car against thieves. Keep valuables out of sight, and don't lock animals in the car without adequate ventilation and something to drink.

The directions given in the text are usually right or left in the direction of travel. Sometimes compass directions, east, west, etc. are given. It is on the walks in this book that children can begin learning how to read maps and use a compass. Never let an opportunity to do so go by.

Distances and height gain are measured, and rounded up or down. Distances are 'Total Distance' for the round trip. Height gain is not always continuous, but reflects the many ups and downs you will face.

KEY TO MAPS

The maps in this book are produced at two scales. One is the scale 1:25000, the other, 1:40000. Distances on these maps are represented as follows:

1:25000 (Walks 1, 2, 3, 4, 5, 6, 7, 8, 10, 13, 14, 15)

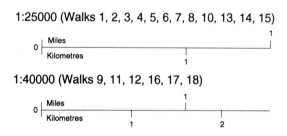

1:40000 (Walks 9, 11, 12, 16, 17, 18)

The following symbols have been used on all maps:

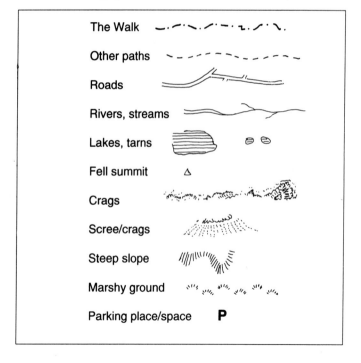

The Walk	
Other paths	
Roads	
Rivers, streams	
Lakes, tarns	
Fell summit	△
Crags	
Scree/crags	
Steep slope	
Marshy ground	
Parking place/space	**P**

BUTTERMERE
and the
VALE OF LORTON

In his *Guide to the Lakes*, Thomas West, writing in 1778, observed of the people of Buttermere: "The life of the inhabitants is purely pastoral. A few hands are employed in the slate quarries; the women spin woollen yarn and drink tea."

This was the dawn of the age of exploration. Few travellers had visited the Lake District, and more often than not, what they recorded was what they saw, untainted by preconceived notions of how things should be. That didn't remain for long, and Buttermere's story often goes no further than the recounting of the tale of the Maid of Buttermere, mentioned in the text. Whether or not the inhabitants drank tea and spun wool, when Captain Joshua Budworth related his experiences at the Fish Inn in Buttermere village, he unleashed on the valley a deluge of curiosity.

Today, with all these fascinating snippets documented and rewritten to the nth degree, Buttermere plays a valuable and positive role in the economy of Lakeland. It still has its tourists, its walkers, picnickers, campers, motorists, mountain bikers, and so on. And it still has its abiding charm and beauty.

In *Days in Lakeland: Past and Present*, E M Ward, writing in 1929, commented: "After Wasdale, Buttermere, but little less remote, seems a dale very flowery and full of trees. The hesitant entry of spring into the vale of Buttermere is, even in these days, troubled but by a cold nor'wester up the lakes or by the chill of a May snowfall on Red Pike and Great Gable. Wild hyacinths on the slopes of the valley behind Rannerdale Knotts brighten day by day, acres and acres of wild hyacinths that no one gathers. Across the dale near the end of Scale Bottom there is a dim pallor, of the same delicate hue as dew on flowering grasses, of the faint blue tinge that lies over screes in a clouded light."

Such sights and observations are still there. The wild hyacinths remain, a dewy sheen still lies across the sleek fellsides, and the beauty that is Buttermere awaits those who care to seek it out.

For greatest impact you must approach Buttermere over the Honister Hause, swiftly leaving behind the remains of man's toil, and descending beneath the frowning gaze of Honister Crag and

Fleetwith Pike. Slowly, as you creep into the dale, the majestic expanse of the valley opens up before you. Sweeping, grassy fellsides, dotted with minor crags and discarded boulders, left by some long-retreated glacier, and the distant shimmer of the lakes.

In an often-quoted, but no less apposite comment, W G Collingwood, said: "Buttermere and Crummock are Nature's art for art's sake." - a singularly appropriate observation. Collingwood, however, preferred the approach into the dale from the Vale of Lorton, and there is much to commend that, too. But the suddenness with which the great valley is laid before you scores points for the approach over Honister, and demonstrates that Buttermere is no poor relation to the valley you will have left behind.

Once into the valley there is no escape until you reach the village of Buttermere, these days the focal point of the valley, and approached by a fine road over Newlands Hause. From this direction, however, you see only the mountains of the High Stile range that backdrop the village, and, as Housman describes in *A Descriptive Tour and Guide to the Lakes, Caves, Mountains and other Natural Curiosities in Cumberland, Westmoreland, Lancashire and a part of the West Riding of Yorkshire* (1808), "a long white strip of water rushing down from the summit of the mountain, known in the neighbourhood by the name of Sour-milk-force...It issues from a small lake...the seite (sic) of which, some imagine, has been the focus of a volcano."

Beyond Buttermere, the valley runs onwards as the Vale of Lorton, relatively free from dizzy heights, more at rest with its fields of sheep, patterned by drystone walls and groups of stone farm buildings. It is outstandingly beautiful, making its own contribution to the walking scene in the Loweswater Fells, a perfect balance to the mountain masses of Robinson, Hindscarth and Dalehead, and the High Stile range.

The walks in this book take a wide sweep across the many available in Buttermere and the Vale of Lorton, and range from brief lakeside strolls, to longer, more demanding outings. The aim is not to inhibit a child's natural curiosity about this magnificent landscape, but to encourage him or her to become part of it, to experience "Nature's art", and to begin the process of learning about hill walking and the British countryside.

WALK 1:
Dalehead from Honister Pass

The underlying rock of Skiddaw Slates gives Dalehead its rounded and easy-to-climb shape when viewed from Honister. From the

Start: Car park, rear of youth hostel, Honister Pass. GR 225135
Total Distance: 3½ km (2 miles)
Height gain: 395m (1295 feet)
Difficulty: Steady ascent on paths of grass, stone and rock. The summit cairn stands close to the edge of a steep drop.

summit cairn the view is especially fine, overlooking the dale of Newlands, and extending to Catbells and the distant purple-blue shape of Skiddaw. Not far from Honister Pass lie the crags and disused quarry workings of Fleetwith Pike, and these are well seen on this walk, as are the summits of Great Gable and Scafell Pike. The significant ascent is a good test of a child's willingness to plod up a steady slope: the view is well worth the effort.

THE WALK:

Leave the car park by the steps next to the slate works (signposted: Great Gable. Dubs Quarry). Cross the road, following a footpath sign, and ascend, keeping the fence on your right, to a step stile. Cross the stile and continue along the fenceline until it ends. When it does, the route is clearly trodden to the summit, which stands by the iron post remains of the old parish boundary fence.

THE WAY BACK:

To return, simply retrace your steps, admiring the fine pros-pect of Honister Crag and Fleetwith Pike en route.

OPTIONAL EXTRA:

In good visibility you can extend the walk by continuing along the ridge - Hindscarth Edge - linking Dalehead with the next summit, Hindscarth. This extra walking will add about 3.5 km (2 miles) to the overall distance, but is most exhilarating.

ALONG THE WAY:

Honister Quarry: *During the Ordovician period (450-500 million years ago), a time of violent volcanic outpourings, the ancient*

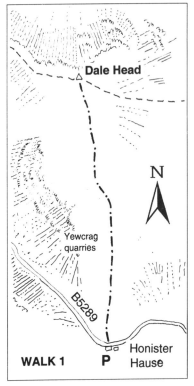

Dale Head

Yewcrag quarries

N

B5289

WALK 1   **P** Honister Hause

take very much for granted was not laid until 1935.

As you ascend the pass by car from Seatoller you can see the old wagon route to the quarry in a few places.

Towards the end of the last century, Herman Prior, author of the Pedestrian and General Guide to the Lake District of England recommended the ascent from the top of Honister Pass "because advantage may be taken of the Buttermere wagonettes any morning." The wagonettes were horse drawn, running on sledges due to the steep ascent and rough descent into Buttermere. The horse drawn wagonettes came to an end with the metalling of the road, when the horses were no longer able to control the wagons on the smoother surface of the steep descent into Buttermere.

Skiddaw Slates were covered by rocks now known as Borrowdale Volcanic. The chemical reaction between the Skiddaw Slates and the volcanic lava produced the green Honister Tuff, which until the mid-1970s was quarried on both sides of the Honister Pass for use as facing stone on buildings and in the production of household ornaments.

The tarmac road crossing Honister Pass which today we

WALK 2:
Fleetwith Pike from Honister Pass

Fleetwith Pike, standing at the very head of Buttermere, has many lines of ascent. This route meanders through the heather along the top of the dramatic Honister Crag, giving outstanding views of the surrounding fells, Honister Pass below, and the remains of the quarrymen's huts nestling into the crags. The walk returns to Honister after visiting Dubs Quarry.

In places the walk comes near the very steep slopes falling to the valley, and here young children especially will need close control.

Start: Car park, rear of youth hostel, Honister Pass. GR 225135
Total Distance: 4 km (2½ miles)
Height gain: 280m (920 feet)
Difficulty: This walk over open, heather-covered fellside is mainly on grassy paths, while the start (and finish) make use of steep quarry roads.

THE WALK:

Leave the car park by the steps next to the slate works (signposted: Great Gable, Dubs Quarry). Turn left and follow the road to a gate into the slate works yard. Cross the yard to a conspicuous broad track climbing the hillside.

Ignore the signposted track on the left, which leads to Great Gable. Instead, at the next junction, bear left and continue to a turning on the right as the track zigzags uphill. Turn right here, and in a short distance you reach an old winch wheel.

The route now lies across the fellside behind the winch wheel, on an indistinct path that is all that remains of a quarry sledge way, and which leads to Black Star Quarry.

From the quarry a wide grassy path may be followed to the summit. but I recommend you leave the path, by heading right, shortly after leaving the quarry, to follow the edge of the crag over the minor top, Black Star.

Leaving Black Star, descend to a small tarn, and by keeping to a path on the left, meander through the heather along the crag's edge to join the main path to the summit.

The view from Fleetwith Pike, over Buttermere dale head, and

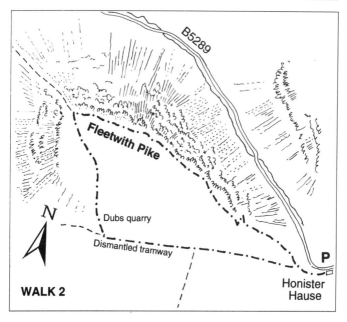

B5289

Fleetwith Pike

Dubs quarry

N

Dismantled tramway

P

Honister
Hause

WALK 2

Crummock Water, on a clear day extends to the Solway Firth, Criffel and the Galloway Hills. To the left rise the fells of Haystacks and High Stile, with the dark, ominous crags of Pillar beyond, while on the right the undulating ridge from Dale Head to Robinson encloses these upper reaches of Buttermere.

THE WAY BACK:

Head southeast from the summit to accompany a broad grassy path across the heather-cloaked hillside, to a small climber's hut at Dubs Quarry. A track heading east between two collapsed walls, an old tramway, is now followed to the site of the Drum House, and then descends steeply (loose in places) to the slate works and Honister Pass.

ALONG THE WAY:

Quarry works: *The small huts nestling in Honister Crag were used by quarrymen (known locally as 'old men'), as living quarters during the week, from where they communicated with their wives by carrier pigeon. Most of the quarrymen lived in the small villages of West Cumberland (as it then was), and would return home on a Saturday evening for a village dance, chapel on Sunday, re-*

turning to work on Monday morning for a 7am start.

Being so high on the crag, the huts were always exposed to wind and rain, and one tale tells how a group of men upon waking in the morning, heard the wind howling, and saw the rain beating against the window. Not surprisingly, they decided to remain indoors, and to forego work for the day. Later, to their cost, they were to find that the water lashing against the window was from a nearby stream, being blown upwards and against the hut by the force of the wind: the penalty was the loss of a day's pay.

Working conditions for the quarrymen were harsh and dangerous. Slate was brought down to the knapping sheds on hurdles, large barrows with two inclining handles (called stangs) at the front, between which the man would position himself, going, like a horse, before the weight. Weighing as much as eighty pounds, it took a man half an hour of laborious effort to carry these contraptions back to the quarry, though the laden descent was often only a matter of minutes, depending on the skill, dexterity and good fortune of the man. The sledging of slate at Honister came to an end in 1881, when a gravitational railway, the course of which we follow from Dubs Quarry, was introduced.

Remarkable tales still abound of men from the 1860s: Samuel Trimmer, who once made fifteen journeys in one day for a bottle of rum and a percentage of the slate he had sledged. And Joseph Clarke of Stonethwaite, who made seventeen journeys and transported almost five tons of slate in one day.

"I get this distinct impression that Fleetwith Pike is regarded as a poor relation amongst the Buttermere Fells, yet it has much to offer. Lakeland's highest youth hostel plus a convenient car-park lie close under its summit. The mountain's gaunt hacked north-eastern face, or Honister Crag as it is more commonly known, with its dizzy galleries and precarious tramways, is a familiar sight to Lakeland's visitors."

Mountain Lakeland
Tom Bowker

WALK 3:

Dubs Quarry via Warnscale Beck

The head of Buttermere is cut into two valleys by the craggy wedge of Fleetwith Pike. On one side lies Gatescarthdale, below the high hanging crags of Honister and its steeply-climbing road into Borrowdale. On the other side, deeply scooped into the hard volcanic rock, hides the valley of Warnscale. The pony trods of Dubs and Green Crag quarries, have long since been abandoned to farmers and walkers, but today provide an excellent way of exploring the rock pools and waterfalls of Warnscale Beck, the crags of Haystacks, and weathered boulders that have been sculpted by wind, ice and rain for thousands of years.

> **Start:** Gatescarth Farm car park. GR 195149
> **Total Distance:** 5½ km (3½ miles)
> **Height gain:** 360m (1180 feet)
> **Difficulty:** Stone and grass paths, rocky outcrops, and unbridged streams

THE WALK:

Leave Gatescarth on the road leading to Honister Hause until you are a short distance past Gatescarth Cottages, and then abandon the road for a stone track on your right (signposted: bridleway). Accompany the track for a little over a kilometre (¾ mile), at which point a stream (sometimes dry) fords the track. Here we depart, right, on a grassy path to cross Warnscale Beck by a wooden bridge.

Follow the quarry track and ascend in a series of zigzags beneath the crags of Haystacks. The cairned path through the crags below the disused buildings of Green Crag quarry, leads you to a junction with a path from Haystacks. Turn left, passing below a rocky crag and descend to cross Warnscale Beck once more. Ascend the grassy bank beyond to reach a small hut on the site of Dubs Quarry.

THE WAY BACK:

The return route is by the track alongside and behind the hut. A well-made quarry track descends with Warnscale Beck cascading far below, passing through the remains of old quarry workings. When Warnscale

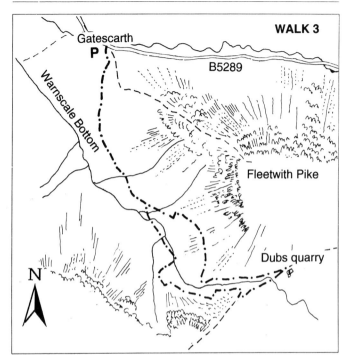

Bottom is reached, follow the track out to Gatescarth.

ALONG THE WAY:

Gatescarth: *Gatescarth is one of the largest Herdwick sheep farms in Lakeland. A hundred years ago it was Edward Nelson who made Gatescarth Herdwick sheep famous, and in later years his son, also Edward, excelled as a breeder of these tough little sheep. In 1934, Edward Nelson died, when the Richardson family from Watendlath took over the farm and continued the farm's great reputation for Herdwicks.*

Gatescarth Cottage: *Until recently, Gatescarth Cottage was lived in by Miss Nelson, daughter of Edward. She had a great understanding of wild animals, and at one time looked after four fox cubs. Two were later given to London Zoo, one left her for a mate in the wild, and was seen over a year later playing with one of his old friends, a sheep dog! The remaining fox lived to the ripe old vulpine age of twelve, when it died of heart failure.*

Warnscale and Dubs Bottom: *The flat pastures of Warnscale Bottom were created over thousands of years by silt washed from the mountain sides. By contrast, the high glacial corrie of Dubs Bottom, now overgrown with vegetation, will at one time have housed a small mountain tarn.*

Dubs Quarry: *The waste heaps of Dubs Quarry intrude on to the marshy corrie of Dubs Bottom, and here quarry workers often lived during the week in small huts, only going home on a Saturday night, and returning on Monday morning. The huts were built from waste stone, without mortar, the two feet thick walls proof enough against both wind and rain. One hut, that visited on this walk, still remains intact, and is used as a climber's hut. This latter-day use of old huts is common throughout the mountainous regions of Britain. As well as providing convenient shelter in poor weather, they play a vital, and often life-saving, role in times of accidents. Always be sure you leave them in the condition in which you find them, or better.*

Fanny Mercer

As you leave Gatescarth Farm your attention is unavoidably drawn to a conspicuous white cross on the steep slopes of Fleetwith Pike. This is the place where a young lady fell to her death in 1887, as a result of tripping over the Victorian equivalent of the modern walker's stick. The cross was erected in Fanny Mercer's memory by her friends.

Such fell-poles, the British version of the trusty alpenstock, were regarded as essential walking equipment during Victorian times, though they had virtually disappeared from Alpine use in Europe by the 1870s, being replaced with the ice-axe.

Coleridge considered himself ill-equipped if he did not have his fell-pole, and is said to have wrestled with his wife for the broom handle on one occasion.

WALK 4:
Haystacks via Scarth Gap

As you drive from Buttermere along the lakeshore towards Honister, Haystacks stands as a rugged interloper amid a ring of high fells.

Start: Gatescarth car park. GR 195149
Total Distance: 7 km (4½ miles)
Height gain: 480m (1575 feet)
Difficulty: In spite of the considerable height gain, this is a pleasant walk on well-maintained paths, making use of a farm track at the start, and finishing by descending a quarry pony trod.

This is truly a fell on which to linger and explore, for nowhere in Lakeland is there so diverse a conglomeration of rocky tors, heather trails, tranquil tarns and outstanding beauty all around.

As a result the ascent of Haystacks is understandably popular, and the summit tarn, on a fine day, a perfect spot for a picnic.

This ascent tackles Haystacks by Scarth Gap, an old pony track linking Buttermere and Ennerdale, and a fine approach to a fine fell.

THE WALK:

A small gate next to the postbox leads the way through Gatescarth Farm to a broad track across the flat expanse of Warnscale Bottom. Beyond, having crossed Warnscale Beck, take a signposted path that leads over to Ennerdale. Rising steeply at first, the path zigzags alongside a fence topped with barbed wire, to a gate. Here the fence falls away to the left, while we continue at a more comfortable gradient to pass through a gap in a wall.

Cairns mark the onward route to Scarth Gap, though paths radiate in many directions. The highest point of the Gap is marked by a large cairn, and here there are numerous small rock outcrops to rest beside, enjoy a break and admire the view.

Once refreshed, leave the Gap by climbing left (east) on a slanting rake, that shortly turns on to a new path wandering through a host of minor outcrops, some of which provide adventurous children with scrambly alternatives to the conventional route - a good path marked by cairns and

19

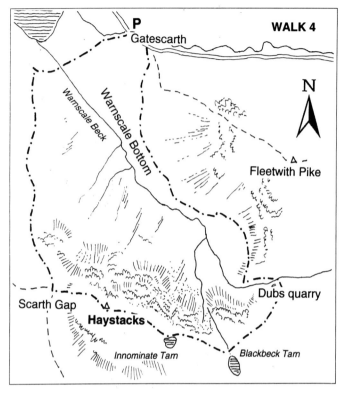

WALK 4

old fence posts. This leads all the way to the summit.

The top of the fell is adorned by a small, dark-eyed tarn, and two iron fence posts at either end of a rocky ridge.

Haystacks is ideally placed among the surrounding and higher fells from which to view them to the best advantage. The summit plateau has many paths snaking through the heather and between rock tors, most finding their way to a nameless tarn, *that has acquired the name Innominate Tarn!*

THE WAY BACK:

Leave the fell top in a southeasterly direction, heading for Innominate Tarn. Pass the tarn, a most beautiful spot, and descend to Black Beck, not far from the outflow of Blackbeck Tarn. Cross the beck and ascend by a grassy path, and soon bear right, around Green Crag. On passing Green Crag look for a large cairn which marks a descending, cairn-lined path that crosses the upper part of Warnscale Beck and joins the pony trod from Dubs Quarry. At this point Warnscale Beck cascades by an attractive series of waterfalls and rock pools to the valley below.

Descend by the track and shortly leave the beck to swing right, across the side of Fleetwith Pike, between hawthorns disfigured by the wind. When you arrive at the once-busy dressing sheds of Dubs Quarry, take to the level track through Warnscale Bottom, enjoying the view down the length of Buttermere on the straightforward return to Gatescarth.

ALONG THE WAY:

Buttermere boundary: *The iron gate at Scarth Gap and the fence posts descending from neighbouring High Crag to cross Haystacks, mark the parish boundary of Buttermere. The present church was built in 1880, but formerly the valley was served by chapels at Gatescarth, Rannerdale, and a site to the north of the present church. These chapels, unable to support a full-time clergyman, were served by a lay-reader, among whom the most famous was 'Wonderful Walker' - Robert Walker (1709-1802) - who served Buttermere until 1736, when he moved to Seathwaite in Dunnerdale. His stipend was 20 shillings a year, supplemented by work as a teacher, labouring, spinning, and taking advantage of the custom known as 'Whittle Gate' under which he was entitled to graze geese on the village common and share the home of each family of the parish for a fortnight or so.*

Haystacks' Eagles

In the issue of *The Gentleman's Magazine*, published in 1751, there is a map of Lakeland with the words 'Here eagles build' across the rocky tors of Haystacks, proof enough, along with nearby Eagle Crag, that eagles did indeed roam widely and freely across the Lakeland landscape. In Borrowdale they used to keep a rope for use as a means of reaching and destroying eagles nests.

This persecution of one of Britain's most majestic and much-maligned birds is now illegal, and eagles have returned to the Lake District after many year's absence.

WALK 5:
Scale Force

Scale Force, the highest of all the Lakeland waterfalls, was the object of considerable admiration among nineteenth-century visitors, who would reach it from Buttermere, though quite a few used to take a shortcut by boat across Crummock Water. The walk, however, is most attractive, and full of interest for young and old minds alike: trout swimming in Buttermere Dubs below Scales Bridge, Herdwick sheep wandering the fellsides, the evocative call of curlew, the distant mewing of a circling buzzard, dippers and grey wagtails flirting busily about the becks, all climaxed by the gushing cataract of Scale Force itself.

Start: Car park, rear of the Fish Hotel. GR 173169
Total Distance: 6½ km (4 miles)
Height gain: 140m (460 feet)
Difficulty: Fairly easy walking on well-defined fell paths and farm tracks, but crossing a few unbridged streams.

Across the expanse of Crummock Water, the Grasmoor massif forms an impressive backdrop, while much closer stands the great green whale of Mellbreak, one of the Loweswater Fells.

THE WALK:
Leave the car park heading for the main road, but turn right to pass in front of the Fish Hotel, and go through a gate. Keep on to a gate on the right (signposted: Scale Bridge, Scale Force) and follow the path beyond it to reach the river, Buttermere Dubs, that links Buttermere and Crummock Water. Cross by a twin-arched stone bridge, Scales Bridge.

Turn right and follow a path to cross first Near and then Far Ruddy Becks. Stay on the path, following a line of cairns across a stretch of wet ground to arrive at a large cairn just past a group of three holly trees.

You have gained a little height by now, and the retrospective view across Buttermere to distant Fleetwith Pike and the dale head is especially pleasing, while across Crummock Water, Rannerdale Knotts and Hause Point stand before the folded crags of Grasmoor.

Bear left, still following a line of cairns, later moving slightly to

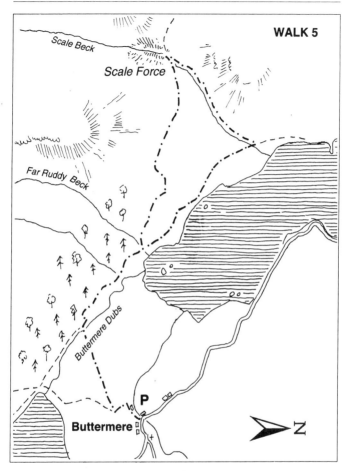

the right as a bouldery path continues below a line of hawthorns.

The onward route, still following cairns, crosses a small stream and another patch of wet ground before reaching a stony path heading for a gap in a wall, beyond which it drops to the bridge immediately below Scale Force.

The bridge is a safe enough vantage point, but, with care, you can venture a little further into the chasm of Scale Beck, but I wouldn't advise this for very young children.

THE WAY BACK:

By way of adding a little variety to the return journey, follow a path going down with the stream, towards the lake. Cross Black Beck by a wooden bridge, and continue past the bracken-covered remains of an ancient settlement, probably all that remains of a small iron works that occupied this convenient site below Scale Force. After a sheepfold turn right across a bridge, and on by a bracken-lined path, heading for a stand of birch trees and another, small bridge. By keeping to the higher ground you will avoid soft wet going, and should head for a conspicuous square-shaped boulder, beyond which a path leads you on towards the lake. By following the path you eventually return to Far Ruddy Beck, from where you can easily retrace your steps to Buttermere.

ALONG THE WAY:

Scale Force: *The highest fall in Lakeland is at its most dramatic following several days of rain; at other times it may be reduced to modest proportions.*

The fall is 38 metres (125 feet) high, and sends Scale Beck into a tree-lined cleft from the high comb above. The scramble into the gorge can be slippery, if wet.

The Fish Hotel: *At the turn of the eighteenth-century, Captain Budworth, author of* A Fortnight's Ramble to the Lakes in Westmoreland, Lancashire and Cumberland *wrote of his stay at the Fish Inn, Buttermere, and of the beauty of the inn-keeper's daughter, Mary. This account caught the eye of a certain John Hadfield, who, posing as the Honourable Alexander Augustus Hope, MP for Linlithgow, wooed and won the 'Beauty of Buttermere', and they were married in Lorton Church on 2nd October 1802.*

Hadfield, alas, was an imposter, already married, and a convicted swindler and confidence trickster, also wanted on a charge of forgery, which in those days carried the death penalty.

For the forgery, Hadfield was tried at Carlisle Assizes, found guilty and hanged.

Mary eventually married a man from Caldbeck, by whom she had seven children, five living into adulthood. When Mary died she was buried in Caldbeck churchyard.

The tale of Mary became the making of much melodrama on the London stage, and for years afterwards tourists invaded Buttermere, the scene of her brief romance with Hadfield.

More recently the story is most evocatively told in Melvyn Bragg's book, The Maid of Buttermere.

WALK 6:
Robinson

This fine, but energetic, ascent of Robinson from Buttermere is a popular walk in spite of the apparently unappetising prospect the fell presents to visitors to Buttermere. The mountain very much dominates the village, and is named after Richard Robinson, a local worthy, who seizing upon the opportunities for landownership suddenly unleashed by Henry VIII's Dissolution of the Monasteries between 1536 and 1539, bought the mountain and the properties that went with it.

Start: Car park, rear of Fish Hotel. GR 173169
Total Distance: 7km (4½ miles)
Height gain: 625m (2050 feet)
Difficulty: Most of the walk is on grassy paths, finishing by a rocky pull to the summit. The way across Buttermere Moss is often wet and tiring. The considerable ascent may prove too much for very young children - and a few adults!

This ascent makes use of an old road, formerly used to bring peat down from Buttermere Moss, that runs high above Newlands Hause, and affords breathtaking views of the surrounding countryside.

The broad, featureless top of Robinson makes this an inappropriate walk in poor visibility.

THE WALK:

Leave the car park, heading for the main road, and climb to the church. Take the road, left, past the church - it continues over into the Newlands valley - and follow it until you reach a small layby on the right. From here, follow a grassy path (signposted) that leaves the road and heads for Robinson, as yet largely unseen.

The path ascends clearly across the head of a gully that plunges to the pass below, and then continues, zigzagging a little to ease the gradient.

Your first objective is the minor top, High Snockrigg, beyond which lies Buttermere Moss and the first sight of Robinson. The path swings right (south) to reach High Snockrigg.

From this mini-fell keep to the

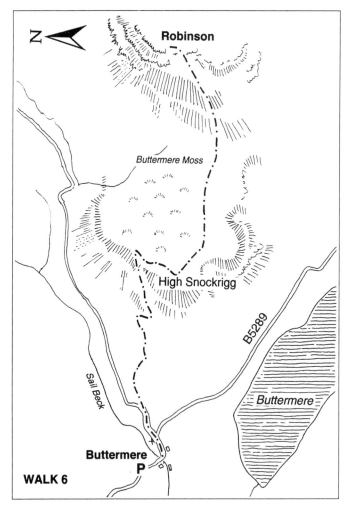

WALK 6

high ground as much as possible across Buttermere Moss, beyond which a cairned track rises to a much larger cairn on the edge of the summit plateau. Keep the position of this large cairn in mind in readiness for the descent.

The top of the fell is stony and largely featureless, but its highest point lies a short walk away to the north, between two small rocky outcrops.

There is a fine feeling of satisfaction on completing this ascent, and on a clear day, the effort is amply rewarded by superb views.

THE WAY BACK:

You return to Buttermere simply by retracing your steps, but take care to ensure you leave the summit plateau at the correct spot, near that large cairn. Come down too soon and you will hit the worst clutches of Buttermere Moss; too late and you will face some very steep and difficult going high above Buttermere lake.

ALONG THE WAY:

Buttermere Church: *The tiny parish church of Saint James, Buttermere, perched on a rocky knoll overlooking the village, is well worth a visit.*

The present church was built in 1880, using stone from Sour Milk Gill, by Reverend Vaughan Thomas of Oxford. Before 1880 there had been a chapel to the north of the present church. Today all that remains of this earlier place of worship are the font and two piers at the entrance to the church enclosure. Although I have found no supporting evidence, there is a claim that an earlier chapel existed in Rannerdale, a short distance away.

The church was extended in 1884, by the addition of a sanctuary at the eastern end, and a vestry to the north. During 1933, Harold Thompson, brother-in-law of the then vicar, designed the west porch with stone from Red Pike across the valley.

Inside the church the simple, but beautifully-carved, font cover was given by the children of Buttermere school in 1930. The school, just below the church, was closed in 1950, but is still in regular use as the village meeting room.

Buzzards

One of the most stirring sights in Lakeland is that of a buzzard circling overhead. Perhaps not everyone would share the view, but the buzzard (*Buteo buteo*) is a characteristic Lakeland bird, nesting on the high crags.

During winter it is not uncommon for buzzards to stay on the high ground, though many descend to the valleys.

Their main food is sheep carrion, and a suspicion that they attacked young lambs led to their persecution during the eighteenth and nineteenth centuries.

WALK 7:
Around Buttermere Lake

"I always think of Buttermere as made by Heaven for summer evenings and summer mornings," wrote W G Collingwood, private secretary to John Ruskin, *"green floor and purple heights."*

Start: Car park at the rear of Fish Hotel, Buttermere. GR 173169
Total Distance: 7 km (4½ miles)
Height gain: 40 m (130 feet)
Difficulty: An easy walk on well-maintained footpaths, farm and forestry access tracks

The walk around Buttermere (you don't really need to add 'lake', but I've done so to distinguish it from the village) can be whatever you want it to be - from a pleasant summer's evening stroll (if 4½ miles isn't 'strolling' too far) to, as so often enjoyed by my own family, a full day of exploration, adventure and picnics at the water's edge.

Nicholas Size used Buttermere as the setting for his story *The Secret Valley* in which he depicts Buttermere as the English headquarters during the Norman invasion of the 1100s.

THE WALK:

Leave the car park and walk round to the front of the Fish Hotel. There follow a farm track (signposted: bridleway) alongside the hotel, and keeping with the track go on through two gates to reach a gated field near the lake's edge.

Go through the gate, and turn right along a hedgerow, leading to a bridge spanning Buttermere Dubs. Cross the bridge, and follow the ensuing path, keeping left to arrive at a small bridge across Sour Milk Gill. The path leads to a gate in a wall, at the lower edge of Burtness Wood, a National Trust property. Through the gate turn left on a forest track (a Permissive Path), running alongside the lake, taking great care not to wander along the steeply ascending path nearby, which leads up to Red Pike, and a lot of hard work.

When the track crosses a stream and climbs to leave the lake, take a footpath on your left.

Along this stretch of lake shore there are fine views across the lake. The prominent white house

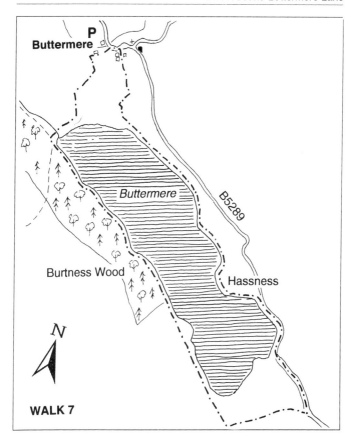

WALK 7

is Hassness, set against a backdrop of the sweeping fellsides of Robinson, dotted with craggy outcrops and tumbled boulders.

Continue to a bridge over a small stream, and then on to a gate in a wall.

Soon, you leave Burtness Wood behind, to continue on a stony fellside path to a bridge spanning Comb Beck, near Horse Close - a small woodland area of larch enclosed by a dry stone wall.

Continue along the path until you reach a wall that leads on to a sheepfold and a gate. Turn left through the gate, cross the bridge over Warnscale Beck, and follow a fenced track to Gatescarth Farm, renowned for its Herdwick sheep.

At the farm, take the gate marked 'Lakeside Path', and follow signs to the road.

Without wishing to encourage dental downfall, this is a spot at which you can usually buy locally-made ice cream, from a van stationed in the car park.

On reaching the road, turn left and cross Gatescarthdale Beck. After about 500 yards, the road bends right, following the lakeshore. Look for a footpath on the left (signposted: Buttermere via Lakeshore Path, Permission by Landowner), and follow this. The path keeps to a line of holly trees, just above the water's edge, and leads to a step stile into an open field.

Now, following the pebbled beach, head for a large tree next to a gate in a wall, and continue along the beach towards a stand of Scots pine, adjoining Crag Wood.

This is an ideal spot for a picnic, with seats, shelter, and shallow water at the lake edge. There is, too, a fine view across the lake to the High Stile range, along which you can pick out the fine glacial corries of Burtness Comb and Bleaberry Tarn.

Pressing on, cross Hassness-how Beck, and enter the wooded grounds of Hassness. Keep to the rocky path, enclosed by trees, to a kissing gate, where a path has been cut into the crag where it plunges 30 feet into the water below - a place where young children will need close control.

The path now disappears into a tunnel, cut through the rock, and brings you out to a gate. Go through the gate on a well-defined gravel path, and cross woodland pasture to a third gate. Here, turn right on a fenced path crossing a traditional Lakeland bridge of slate slabs. The path continues around another rocky outcrop to a gate in the wall above.

Go through the gate and follow a path (signposted: Footpath Buttermere village. Turn left 100 yards) to Wilkinsyke Farm.

Go through the farmyard to reach the road, and there turn left to the Bridge Hotel and the car park.

ALONG THE WAY:

Geology: *The glacial erosion which deepened Buttermere and Crummock Water, then as one lake, occured more than 20,000 years ago. At that time, the Lake District, Scotland and North Wales resembled present-day Greenland, a massive dome of ice.*

The greatest erosion was caused by a large valley glacier, while high on the adjoining fells, tributary glaciers have cut back deeply into the volcanic rock to create the hanging valleys of Burtness Comb and Sour Milk Gill, with typically steep headwall cliffs. Robinson and Dalehead are made of softer Skiddaw Slates, which give the north side of the valley a smoother profile.

The name Buttermere means 'the lake beside the pastures', a reference to the flat farmland between the two lakes, which was formed by deltas of silt washed down by Sour Milk Gill and Sail Beck over thousands of years.

The Tunnel: *During the nineteenth-century, George Benson, a Manchester mill owner, owned the Hassness Estate. He it was who had the tunnel made, both to keep his estate workers busy during the winter months, and to enable him to walk around the water's edge without the need to climb over the crag through which the tunnel is built.*

On reaching Buttermere

(Housman's *Guide to the Lakes*, 1808)

"A legion of rugged mountains in front, whose pointed summits have long been in view, runs across the end of this vale; as we approach their bases, which are deeply entrenched on the opposite side of the vale, they appear still higher, and rise in Alpine forms, with dark and gloomy aspects, known to the shepherds by the names of Hay-cock, High-crag, High-stile, and Red-pike.-Just over the little village of Buttermere, which now opens to the view at the bottom of the vale, we see a long white strip of water rushing down from the summit of the mountain, known in the neighbourhood by the name of Sour-milk-force, which falls some hundreds of yards in almost perpendicular descent. It issues from a small lake, singularly placed in the upper regions of High-crag and High-stile, the scite of which, some imagine, has been the focus of a volcano. This elevated lake, called Burtness-tarn*, is not without its finny inhabitants, trout being found there in considerable quantities."

* For "Burtness-tarn", now read Bleaberry Tarn

These wonderfully descriptive accounts of visits to the Lake District, often portraying the awesome nature of the landscape, are typical of the period.

WALK 8:

Cinderdale Common to Buttermere

This delightful walk, through one of the most scenic valleys in the northwestern lakes visits the little known region of Rannerdale and

Start: Cinderdale Common car park, adjoining Cinderdale Beck. GR 162193
Total Distance: 7 km (4½ miles)
Height gain: 180 m (590 feet)
Difficulty: An easy walk, mainly on grassy paths, rocky in places, and rising gently. A small amount of road walking; some wet stretches and small unbridged streams

High Rannerdale, National Trust property, but actively farmed. There are numerous places to stop for a picnic, or a choice of pubs in Buttermere for a bar meal.

The scenery is of the highest order throughout, with especially fine views of Crummock Water, Buttermere and the surrounding fells. In springtime, the ground is awash with bluebells, while in autumn the changing colours of bracken and deciduous woodlands contrast vividly with the purple-hued heather growing among the crags and across the fellsides. With such unrivalled beauty all around, Rannerdale possesses a pervading aura of tranquility.

THE WALK:

At the head of the car park is a farm track leading on to the fellside, follow it, turning right to ford Cinderdale Beck. *(If the beck is in spate, cross by the road bridge and follow the opposite side of the beck to the ford, rejoining the track there.*

Follow the track across a dried up stream bed to a small outcrop above Rannerdale Farm. Continue to a gate and step stile. A short way further on a sign di-

rects you to a wooden bridge spanning Rannerdale Beck. Cross the bridge, and head for a gate in a dry stone wall. Through the gate, turn left to follow a distinct track climbing easily through High Rannerdale, keeping the wall on your left. When the wall ends, the track crosses a wet area and a small stream; continue ahead to a col between Rannerdale Knotts and Whiteless Breast.

From the col, turn towards

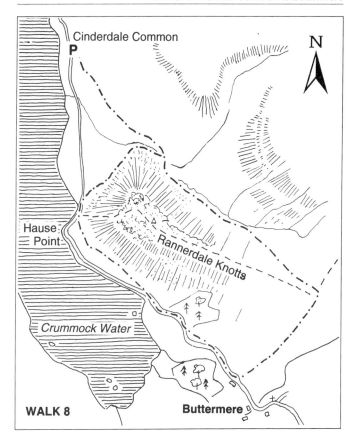

Buttermere, and descend a grassy path through bracken. After crossing a wet patch, bear left to a gate, and continue along a track behind Crag Cottages to the road.

At this point you might want to take a break, perhaps to head into Buttermere for a meal, later retracing your steps.

Continue by following the road towards Crummock Water for about 300 yards. Then take an ungated stony track on your right, passing a small woodland of beech and larch. The track descends to rejoin the road, and continues round a bend, beyond which you take a signposted bridleway on your right.

This track rises above Hause Point, with its fine view over the lake, and then descends in zigzags to the road once more. Turn right, to reach a car park.

Walk through the car park, and, keeping to the left wall, shortly reach a gate. Through the gate, follow the remains of a stone wall which lead you back to the bridge over Rannerdale Beck, from where you can easily retrace your steps to Cinderdale Common.

ALONG THE WAY:

Cinderdale Common *derives its name from the smelting which went on in the area, the cinders from which were tipped on the common.*

Geology: *The numerous rock outcrops through Rannerdale show examples of slump fold formations in the Skiddaw Slate rock. Slump folds were created in the layers of volcanic ash which settled as mud in ancient seas. Between the time of deposition and the end of the Caledonian period, these layers were folded many times, faulted and metamorphosed by heat.*

Rannerdale: *The valley of Rannerdale holds a place in history, romantically related in Nicholas Size's book* The Secret Valley. *The story relates, among other things, how the men and women of Buttermere repelled the Normans at the end of the eleventh-century. Earl Boethar had been leading the people of Lakeland, using Buttermere as his secret base.*

The Normans made many attempts to enter Buttermere via Newlands and Honister, without success, finally deciding to attempt an invasion from Cockermouth in the north. Anticipating the Normans' plan, Earl Boethar had the road over Hause Point concealed, and a new false road laid into Rannerdale.

As the Norman army approached, Boethar's archers fell back into Rannerdale, drawing the Normans away from the lakeshore. Once the Norman army was enclosed within the valley, Boethar's men attacked from both sides and the rear. When all was quiet, the mounds of Norman dead left Rannerdale looking like a charnel-house.

Today, as you travel peacefully into Rannerdale, you will see nothing to tell of this momentous time, save an extensive spread of the most intensely-vivid bluebells. Perhaps, as Terry Marsh observes in The Lake Mountains, *there is something in Omar Khayyám's notion that: 'the loveliest flowers may spring from some dead Caesar's breast.'*

WALK 9:
Around Crummock Water

Crummock Water is twice as long as Buttermere, and possesses some outstandingly beautiful shorelines, along with an attractive grouping of small islands near the lake head. Along with Buttermere

Start: Scalehill Bridge car park. GR 149215
Total Distance: 14½ km (9 miles)
Height gain: 240 m (785 feet)
Difficulty: Mixed walking, covering forestry and farm tracks, grassy and stony fellside paths, and crossing a number of unbridged streams. Boggy in places.

and Loweswater, it once formed one massive glacial lake, subsequently parted by debris brought down from the high fells that surround the lakes.

Without question, Crummock is Grasmoor's lake, setting itself apart from Buttermere, though green-domed Mellbreak, being much closer, might have something to say about that.

The name of the lake derives from the Celtic, cromach, *a crook, so, the crooked lake, which indeed it is, being forced to bend by the impudence of rocky Hause Point. This is one of Lakeland's deepest lakes, and was once renowned for its char, which found its way into such popular Lakeland delicacies of the seventeenth- and eighteenth-century as potted char and char pie.*

Now Crummock Water sees fewer visitors than its near neighbour, though no one can travel its eastern road, especially approaching from the north, without being impressed by Crummock's setting. To walk around the entire lake, no modest undertaking, ranks with the finest valley walks in the Lake District.

THE WALK:
SCALEHILL BRIDGE TO
BUTTERMERE

Leave the car park on a forest track into Lanthwaite Wood, following the course of the River Cocker. Pass through a gate, and proceed to a forked junction. Take the right branch for about 100 yards, and then continue ahead, passing a single bar gate, to the boat house on the lake shore.

Cross the shingle behind the

boat house, and take a path through a young plantation, crossing three step stiles to arrive at a gate leading to an open field. Keep with the lake edge across another step stile, then follow a fence (on your left) to reach a field owned by the National Trust, known as Fletcher Field.

The National Trust are particularly active around all the lakes of Buttermere and the Vale of Lorton, gradually increasing the native hardwoods, planting predominantly oak.

After crossing a small stream the onward path courts the lake's edge to arrive at a wall. Turn left, climbing a flight of steps to a gate leading on to the road.

Turn right, along the road, and head for the car park on Cinderdale Common, crossing the common to a farm track fording Cinderdale Beck.

Throughout the whole of this section of the walk you feel the presence of the great dark bulk of Grasmoor. Its 852 metres don't put it in the Lakeland 'Top Twenty' fells on height alone, but for many experienced fellwalkers it is one of the district's most rewarding summits.

Beyond Cinderdale Beck follow the track across a dried up stream bed, and keep going to a gate and step stile. A little further on a sign directs you to a wooden bridge spanning Rannerdale Beck.

Cross the beck and turn right to follow the remains of a wall to a gate. As you go through the gate, the crags of Rannerdale Knotts seem to bar forward progress, but keep on to reach a small parking area, and then the road.

Turn left, and a short distance along the road towards Hause Point, leave it for a broad grassy track on the left (signposted: Bridleway), which zigzags across the shoulder of Hause Point. On the subsequent descent towards Buttermere, the views across the valley, of the High Stile range, and distant Fleetwith Pike at the head of the valley, are quite breathtaking.

As you reach the road go round a bend to a stony track, and here turn left, passing a small woodland of larch and beech. When you rejoin the road, follow it left, to Buttermere village.

BUTTERMERE TO SCALE FORCE

The next stage of the walk leads around Crummock Water to Scale Force. This part of the route is described in detail in Walk 5, to which I would ask you to refer.

SCALE FORCE TO SCALEHILL BRIDGE

From Scale Force follow the beck

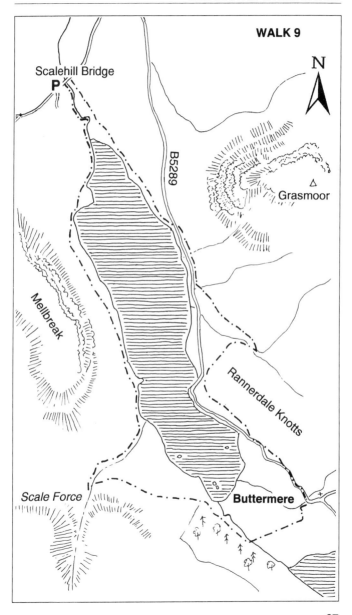

downstream towards the lake, and passing the bracken-covered remains of an old settlement. So far this section of the walk matches the return route for Walk 5, but when you pass the settlement and a sheepfold take a path going left (northwards) along the lake shore, on the final stage of the walk.

Soon, you pass Low Ling Crag, a small rocky island sticking out into Crummock Water, and connected by a shingle strand.

Along the next section countless minor streams flow down from Mellbreak, on your left, and the going is, as a result, invariably wet. When the level of Crummock Water is low it becomes possible to walk along the shingle margin, though not long after passing Low Ling Crag you can opt for a slightly higher path for just under a mile. Either way, high or low, the objective is a gap in a wall next to the lake.

Cross two stiles and turn left along a derelict wall to the remains of a Peel tower, most of the stone that once formed it having been used in the surrounding walls. Continue to a group of Scots pine, and there cross a stile on to a concrete flood barrier, which is now used to reach an hexagonal building, a pump house.

Follow the flood barrier crossing Park Beck to the fish ladder and outflow into the River Cocker, an impressive sight when the water levels are high.

Cross two wooden bridges and turn left to pursue a riverside path back to the car park.

ALONG THE WAY:

Crummock Water *today supplies the water needs of the Workington area of West Cumbria. At the turn of the century, Workington Corporation carried out work on sluice gates to maintain the lake's water level. Today, the water treatment works are in the care of North West Water, while the lake and much of the surrounding land are in the custody of the National Trust.*

Hause Point: *Strange as it may seem, the track over Hause Point, met with about a third of the way around this walk, used to be the main route into Buttermere before a road was forced around it. As you cross the Point you can still see the cart wheel marks etched into the rock.*

Peel Tower: *Peel (or Pele) Towers date from the late Middle Ages, and might be looked upon as an expression of the uncertainties of existence in those troubled times. They are most common in Scotland, Northumberland and Ireland, and acquired the name because they consisted of a central living tower within a peel or pale, i.e. a stock-*

ade, usually of earth and logs. In later structures the stockade was built of stone.

The peel tower near Crummock Water, which in Nicholas Size's book The Secret Valley *is portrayed as a supply depot for the people of Buttermere during the* Norman invasions in the eleventh century, most probably is later than that, dating from the times of the Border reivers, who penetrated far south, rustling cattle until the Union of the Crowns in 1603.

Herdwick sheep

The typical Lakeland fell farm runs a small milking herd, usually Friesians, which in summer grazes the dale pastures and in winter stays indoors in the shippons. The sheep in summer graze the highest intakes and the unenclosed fell commons all the way up to the mountain summits. The flocks are brought down in late November, early December for mating, after which some of the breeding ewes stay on the lower ground, while others, and the non-breeding sheep, return to the lower fells for the winter.

The native breed of sheep is the Herdwick, a small coarse-woolled animal of great hardiness and agility (the local expression is 'terrible lish'). The Herdwick has a strong homing instinct which contrives to keep it on its own ground, or heaf, on the unenclosed fells, but the local farmers are very experienced at managing flocks on unenclosed land. Each farm has its own mark, a combination of coloured daubs on the fleece and a particular nick in the ear - the smit mark and the lug mark respectively - which is recorded in the local 'Shepherd's Guide' and is used to identify strays.

The gathering-in of wide-ranging flocks can only be done with the help of sheepdogs, which in the Lake District are usually the local sort of Border collie. Television has brought the work of these marvellous animals to many people, but they may also be seen in action at the summer Sheepdog Trials, notably at Rydal and Troutbeck, and at the many agricultural shows that feature throughout the region.

WALK: 10

Rannerdale Knotts

This short walk to the top of Rannerdale Knotts is a good way of introducing young members of the family to country walking.

The route makes a circular tour that is well-endowed with fine views of the surrounding fells and of Buttermere and Crummock Water. A craggy crest with numerous small outcrops provide interest and diversion, as well as ample opportunity to relax.

Start: Car park rear of Fish Hotel, Buttermere. GR 173169
Total Distance: 4½ km (3 miles)
Height gain: 265m (870 feet)
Difficulty: Grassy paths and tracks, finishing with a rocky crest to the summit.

THE WALK:

Leave the car park and walk up to the road and the Bridge Hotel. Turn left and cross Sail Beck, following the road to Crag Cottages, the last row of cottages on the right. Take a broad path that runs behind the cottages (signposted), go through a wooden gate and along a fenceline. Shortly after you reach a wall, bear left to ascend a grassy path through bracken and rocky outcrops.

The climb continues easily to a col, known locally as Surprise View, and with good reason. Onward, the way lies along the undulating ridge to the left, and leads to a cairn-topped craggy mound that has many of the qualities of the higher fells that surround it. The main summit of the ridge lies a short distance further along the ridge, so, descend to a minor col before the final, short pull to the summit. Once more the views are outstanding.

THE WAY BACK:

The return to Buttermere begins by retracing your steps to the nearby col from where a line of cairns marks a grassy path down to a stony gully leading to the bridleway across Hause Point, at one time the main route into the valley.

On reaching the bridleway, turn left and go down to the road. As the road bends right, leave it for a stony track on the left, which simply short circuits the road for a while, rejoining it further on.

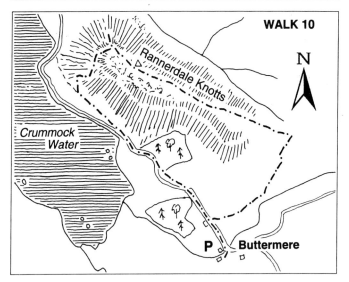

Stay on the road, between iron fences and stone walls, to a gate on your right leading into the wooded area of Long How. Go through the woodland to reach the shore of Crummock Water near a bridge spanning Sail Beck.

Cross the beck and turn left, following a path never far from the stream, back to the car park.

ALONG THE WAY:

Rannerdale Knotts: *Nicholas Size portrayed Rannerdale Knotts in* The Secret Valley *as a command vantage point during the Battle of Rannerdale, which resulted in the massacre of countless Norman invaders.*

No clear account remains of the battle, since in those days *most records were kept by monks, and many of those were in the employ of the Normans.*

The Bridge Hotel: *The Bridge Hotel stands on a site where in the eleventh-century a bakery and armoury stood. Further upstream, among the trees, a water mill supplied the bakery with flour, and for seven centuries the mill and bakery worked continually, the buildings being renewed many times.*

In 1734, the buildings were sold to the church. At that time the curate was Robert Walker, styled the 'Wonderful Walker'. He contrived to obtain a beer licence, an odd thing for a minister to do, and originated the Bridge Inn. Between 1837 and 1845 major rebuilding of the inn

41

took place, using stone from the redundant water mill. When, in 1850, Queen Victoria visited Buttermere, the inn was renamed the 'Victoria' to mark the occasion.

Over the years, many more changes were made, but it was Nicholas Size who largely extended and improved the building. On his death the new owner changed its name back to 'The Bridge'. As demand grew, so both the Bridge and the Fish inns prospered and grew into hotels. At the turn of the twentieth century a new hotel was built, the 'Buttermere', and for many years was known as 't'top hus'.

When is a lake not a lake?

It could be argued that the only true 'lake' in the Lake District is Bassenthwaite Lake; all the others being 'meres' or 'tarns' or 'waters'. Since a 'mere' is by definition a 'lake' or a 'pond', it would be wrong to speak of 'Lake' Buttermere, or Crummock Water Lake.

Whatever you want to call the them, there is no question that what makes the Lake District different from any other mountain district of Britain is its innumerable and varied sheets of water. These exist because of the way glaciers of local origin carved the rocky valleys into basins, and then deposited debris in such a way as to alter the natural drainage of the valley.

So, what is the difference between a lake, and a tarn? You can argue about size for as long as you like, but you won't reach a clear definition there. Loweswater, on the northern edge of the area covered by this book, is undoubtedly a lake. Yet Devoke Water, is not dissimilar in size, but is commonly regarded as a tarn. Clearly, size is not the key factor.

Fortunately, the biologists have contrived a distinction that seems to hold good: it is all to do with plantlife. Apparently, in a lake the characteristic plant is the common reed, while in tarns it is the bottle sedge. Since they both look similar to the untrained eye, all you have to do now is discover how to tell them apart.

WALK 11:
Newlands Hause to Rigg Beck

You need to decide at the start how you are going to tackle this walk. Being linear, it requires a car at each end, or a patient parent prepared to pass away the day peacefully at Newlands Hause before driving down to Rigg Beck to collect the wanderers. Or a driving member of the group willing to return from Knott Rigg to collect the car, while everyone else continues down to Rigg Beck.

Start: Newlands Hause. GR 193176
Finish: Rigg Beck. GR 229201
Total Distance: 5½ km (3½ miles)
Height gain: 305 m (1000 feet)
Difficulty: A fine grassy ridge walk, starting with a short pull. The descent is steep, and can be slippery when wet. Unbridged Rigg Beck needs to be crossed near the end.

The complete traverse is well worthwhile, and a better walk than simply retreating from Knott Rigg, but you do need to solve the transportation difficulties.

The walk is an excellent outing for young and old alike, and though the ascent of Knott Rigg calls for a little effort, the rewards are satisfying indeed.

THE WALK:

From the off-road parking area at Newlands Hause a small wooden signpost directs you uphill (east of north), over springy turf, on to an obvious path which clambers energetically to the ridge above. Once the initial steepness is overcome, the onward walk to the first summit, Knott Rigg, is quite easy.

The summit, a large grassy expanse dotted with slate outcrops, is marked by a small cairn, from which you can see the ridge running on to Ard Crags, set against the backdrop of Sail, Scar Crags and shapely Causey Pike.

As you leave the summit, take care to trend to the left, to avoid a second ridge descending to Keskadale Farm.

Gradually the path drops to a shallow col, with a fine view down Ill Gill (on the right) to the Newlands Valley. Ascend the grassy ridge beyond to reach

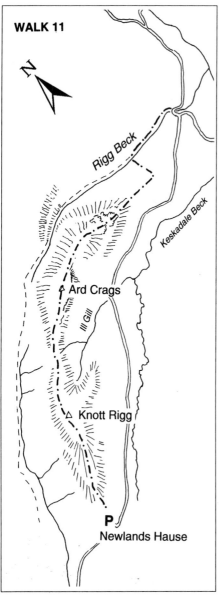

WALK 11

N

Rigg Beck

Keskadale Beck

Ard Crags

Ill Gill

△ Knott Rigg

P

Newlands Hause

the second summit, Ard Crags. Either side of the ridge, the descending fellside is clad in heather, with only the occasional birch tree to introduce a note of change.

The grassy top of Ard Crags is soon reached, a small cairn marking the highest point.

Descend on a grassy path for about 500 yards and then change direction to wander down to the rocky outcrops of Aikin Knott, a mini-summit. Take care as you descend, especially after rain.

The path passes through bracken to a wall corner and a gate, where a sign directs you to the left, downhill, alongside a fence and wall, to cross Rigg Beck by stepping stones.

On the other side of the beck, a good path leads you, right, to the valley road, where there is a small parking area, and, hopefully, someone to pick you up.

ALONG THE WAY:

Knott Rigg: *The waters of Knott Rigg all feed the River Derwent. To the east they flow by Keskadale Beck and Newlands Beck into Bassenthwaite Lake, then by the River Derwent to reach the sea at Workington.*

To the west, the streams flow into Sail Beck and Crummock Water, leaving as the River Cocker, and meeting the Derwent at Cockermouth.

Walls and fences: *Many of the valley rivers and becks are spanned, between walls and fences, by water gates. These, like the walls and fences, are used to control their flocks. The gates are not made to take a person's weight, and should not be used as a means of crossing a river.*

Newlands Hause

Newlands Hause is a gateway through the mountains between the Vale of Keswick and the Buttermere valley. For most visitors it is a charming spot, the opportunity to potter about on the lower slopes of Knott Rigg, and to inspect the cascades of Moss Beck.

If you look more closely, and compare the two sides of the valley, you cannot fail to be impressed by a significant difference in the terrain. To the west, the long sweeping fellsides above Sail Beck lead upwards to the crag-girt summits of Wandope and Sail, scenery that is the hallmark of Skiddaw Slates country, the oldest rocks in Lakeland. The craggy tops are formed from the Borrowdale Volcanic Series, mere striplings on the geological timescale, compared with the Skiddaw Slates. Noticeable, too, is the absence of the customary network of drystone walls, clear evidence that the landscape descended from a medieval deer forest of the sixteenth-century to the common pastures of lowland farms.

To the east, looking above Moss Force, you can see how the Skiddaw Slates, here facing north and so retaining snow and ice much longer, have been scooped into corries that form deep scars.

WALK 12:
Gasgale Gill, Coledale Hause and Whiteless Pike

An opportunity to tackle a major summit and a fair amount of ascent, on one of the finest circular walks in the Western Fells. This walk begins beside the delightful cascades and pools of Gasgale Gill, which it follows to Coledale Hause, a wide expanse of high mountain pasture.

Start: Lanthwaite Green. GR 158207
Total Distance: 11½ km (7 miles)
Height gain: 655m (2150 feet)
Difficulty: A sustained mountain walk on stony paths, with 5 km (3 miles) of continuous, steady ascent. The connecting ridge between Wandope and Whiteless Pike is not difficult, but is fairly narrow.

Combined with a visit to Wandope, which has a surprisingly impressive view, and the narrow grassy ridge of Whiteless Pike, this walk would be a good way of assessing a young child's ability to cope with a longer walk, with more sustained uphill walking.

The potentially confusing nature of Coledale Hause, counsels against tackling the walk in poor visibility - in any case, the views, and the stirring scenery, number among the many reasons for visiting this popular part of Lakeland.

THE WALK:

Begin from the car park at Lanthwaite Green and cross the road to gain a broad green path to a wooden bridge spanning Gasgale Gill. Here turn right on a clear path to scramble over a rock outcrop.

The onward route now quite simply follows the course of Gasgale Gill, a stony proposition, with splendid cascades and rocky pools all the way to Coledale Hause.

The walk to Coledale Hause alone is a superb outing, sandwiched between the massive bulk of Grasmoor on the right, and the soaring fellsides and crags of Whiteside on the left.

When the path reaches Coledale Hause, it does so a little higher than the lowest point, but this is not a cause for con-

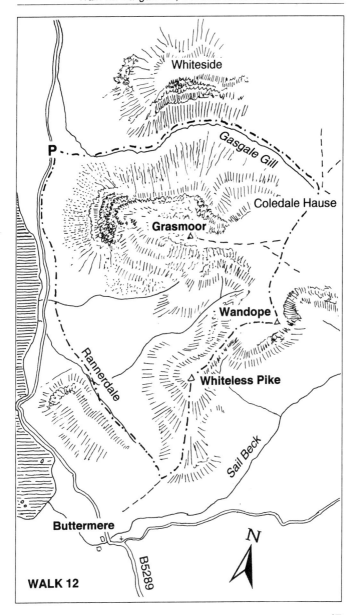

WALK 12

cern, since it simply sets you off in the correct direction.

Back across the Hause you can see the shapely peak of Grisedale Pike, and to its left, Hopegill Head. In front of you, returning to your direction of travel, the rocky scree slopes rise to Crag Hill, part of a splendid high mountain circuit known as the Grisedale Horseshoe.

Returning to the task in hand, climb away from Coledale Hause on a clear, stony path between Crag Hill (left) and the grassy slopes of Grasmoor, to meet a path at a higher col.

From this col, set off half left (southeast), up easy grassy slopes to the flat top of Wandope, the highest point of the walk, and the last of the continuous uphill walking. A narrow path heads you in the right direction from the col, but eventually disappears. When it does, keep ascending to arrive at a small cairn close by a steeply descending edge. Keep very young children in close control here.

Congratulations are in order at this point, especially for any child making their first real ascent of a Lakeland fell. The view, many would say, is reward enough, quite breathtaking. To your left, the corrie and crags of Addacomb Hole are superb, its beck usually a dashing white slash down the fellside to Sail Beck far below.

On the continuing route, now is the time you realise why I advised against tackling this walk in poor visibility!

The on-going ridge to Whiteless Pike is difficult to locate in poor visibility. To make matters worse, closer to the summit of Wandope a second ridge descends...but only to the wrong valley, far below. In good visibility, this problem can be avoided quite easily.

Leave Wandope's summit heading west, and being constantly vigilant not to follow the wrong ridge. Whiteless Edge is quite narrow and distinctive, and leads down to a neat col, Saddle Gate. Beyond a large cairn, known as Thirdgill Head Man, but not shown on maps, marks the start of the fine traverse of Whiteless Edge, culminating in a final, agreeable short pull, skirting rock outcrops, to Whiteless Pike's summit cairn.

From Whiteless Pike, a stony path zigzags down to Whiteless Breast, there changing direction to reach a col at the head of Rannerdale, at Surprise View.

Turn right from the col, descending into Rannerdale. Lower down, the path crosses a boggy stretch, and Squat Beck to reach a wall. Keep the wall on your right and continue to a small gate through the wall. Go through this and cross Rannerdale Beck by a wooden bridge. Climb left to gain a grass farm track leading to Cinderdale Common. Ford Cinderdale Beck (or go down to the road), cross the common to the road, and follow this below the towering crags of Grasmoor back to Lanthwaite Green.

ALONG THE WAY:

Herdwick Sheep: *Most of the sheep you are likely to see on the fells are Herdwicks, a tough and independent breed, that form the major source of income for the local farmers. The hardiest of all sheep breeds, Herdwicks are able to withstand the harsh conditions of the Cumbrian fells, and have probably been farmed here for more than 1000 years. The sheep were a popular breed with monastic farming communities, especially during the twelfth-century, and were probably introduced by Norse and Irish settlers.*

A Memorable Water-Spout

Without the rain the lakes and tarns of the Lake District would be bone dry. Rain, in moderation, you can cope with, but from time to time the Lake District sees some formidable deluges. One of the most recent was in 1966, when Stockley Bridge in Borrowdale was washed away.

"On September 9, 1760, a 'memorable water-spout' descended upon Grasmoor. From the slopes of the mountain a new-born river rushed down towards Crummock Lake, a stream described as five or six yards deep and nearly a hundred yards across. With it it bore immense masses of rock, earth, and rubble torn from the mountain, which were spread out fanwise on the lowest slopes above Lanthwaite Green in a 'dry delta'."

Days in Lakeland: Past and Present
E M Ward

WALK 13:
Nether How

This pleasant short walk to the wooded shore of Crummock Water passes through the congenial oak woodlands of Long How, a National Trust property. Nether How is a neat, wooded mound overlooking the lake, and an ideal spot for a picnic - kind days in spring or autumn, when the valley is a little quieter, are best.

Start: Long How car park. GR 173172
Total Distance: 2 km (1¼ miles)
Height gain: 40 m (130 feet)
Difficulty: Easy; a pleasant walk through woodland, and along field paths.

THE WALK:

Leave the car park by the corner gate and enter the oak woodland of Long How. The path soon joins a vehicle track. Turn left along this until it swings right, uphill. Here, take a path descending to the stream below, Sail Beck. Now follow the beck to a wooden bridge, cross it, and turn right (signposted) along a path leading you out to Nether How and the shore of Crummock Water.

Near the lake shore, the stile over the fence on the right leads on to land over which the National Trust have negotiated access agreements.

THE WAY BACK:

To find your way back, return to the bridge over Sail Beck, where you are faced with a choice of routes. Either, cross the bridge and retrace your steps to the car park, or, without crossing the bridge, take a field path alongside the beck, heading upstream towards Buttermere village.

Near a watergate, go through a small gate, and keep a wire fence on your right to reach a bridge across the beck, into a camping field. Go past the bridge, keeping to a path leading to a gate into the National Park car park at the rear of the Fish Hotel.

Keep on through the car park to reach the road near the Bridge Hotel. Turn left to cross Mill Bridge, and follow the road for the short distance back to Long How car park.

ALONG THE WAY:
Oak woodlands: *The oak wood-*

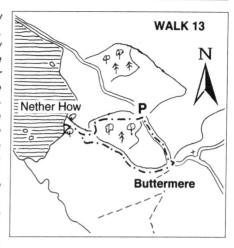

lands of Long How and Nether How, along with many other stretches of the valley, are owned or managed by the National Trust, using methods which maintain or improve the environment to help wild life. Birds take great advantage of this, and passing through the woodland you will invariably see chaffinch, blue and great tit, or the elusive treecreeper, a shy bird that climbs mouse-like up a tree trunk in search of insects, spiralling around the tree until it reaches the top, and then flying down to the base of the next one to begin the process again.

Along the beck you may well see grey wagtails, grey above and yellow/white below. Often they perch on beckside rocks, which is when you will see why they are called wagtails. Look, too, for the occasional dipper, a small black bird with a distinctive white chest, that patrols the streams of Lakeland.

Hows: *In Lakeland folklore the name 'how' usually signifies a small hill used as a burial ground, and dates from the Middle Ages. In Buttermere and the Vale of Lorton, it is said that many of*

these small hills date from the time of the Norman invasions in the eleventh-century. The English dead would be buried on a small hill, or how, while, rather gruesomely, the Norman dead were left where they fell, as a warning to others.

WALK 14:

Stanger Spa

Visiting a once-famous, but now disused Lakeland spa, this easy walk tours field paths and farm tracks, with hedgerows that in springtime are filled with birdlife and wild flowers.

Start: Layby, 50m from Southwaite Bridge. GR 131283
Total Distance: 4½ km (3 miles)
Height gain: 65m (210 feet)
Difficulty: Easy, but all field boundaries are flanked by barbed wire. There are twelve stiles in total on this walk, some without a gated alternative. The walk would therefore prove unsuitable for anyone unable to climb over ladder stiles.

THE WALK:

Walk along the road (east) away from the bridge to a signposted footpath across the fence on your right. Head for a wooden footbridge across a small beck, and ascend among hawthorn bushes alongside a reed-filled gully, the line of an old farm track. When you reach a gate, go through it, and keep along the hedgerow beyond to a stile and gate. Cross the stile, and with the hedgerow now on your right, head towards a gate leading on to a road.

Turn right along the road to Low Stanger and Stanger Farms, where a signposted bridleway directs you to Lorton. Go past this sign, and turn left on another bridleway between farm buildings. After the first building you are confronted with a large NO ENTRY sign. Here, take a path on your right (signposted) to a gate. Through the gate, turn left to another gate, leaving the farms along a track leading to a gate into a field. From this point the route to Stanger Spa is waymarked by blue arrows on a yellow background.

Go through the gate and keep to the left boundary, along a holly hedgerow. At a fence, cross a stile and continue to a field corner. Turn right to a gate and stile, and continue to a ruined building you can see a short distance away, across wet ground.

The ruined building is Stanger Spa, standing on dry ground, and surrounded by birch trees. The interior of the building is usually filled with water, while a

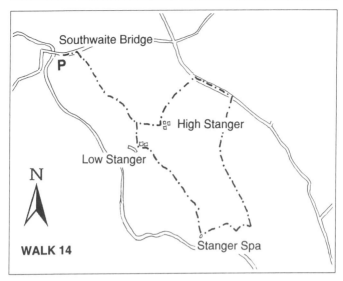

Southwaite Bridge

P

High Stanger

Low Stanger

N

WALK 14

Stanger Spa

square enclosure near the building surrounds the spa spring.

Leave the spa by the nearby gate into a field. Turn left along a birch hedgerow. Follow the hedge to a stile, and then follow a large slate stone wall. At the wall end turn left and follow a fence to a cage wicket gate, beyond which you cross a field, heading for a gate near a stone wall, with a water trough nearby.

Cross a series of stiles, to a wicket gate at the end of a slate wall. Beyond the gate, go right towards a large tree in the middle of the field, then to a wooden gate in the far left field corner, leading on to a road.

Turn left along the road (north-west) for 300 yards to a sign on the left for High Stanger Farm.

Follow the ensuing track almost to the farm where a sign directs you right, across a traditional slate bridge to a stile next to an iron gate. As you cross the stile, keep the hedge on your left and head towards sheep pens. Cross the access track that leads to Low Stanger Farm, and retrace your steps to Southwaite Bridge.

ALONG THE WAY:

Hedgerows: *In most Lakeland areas the hedgerows are a mix of different bushes and trees. Along this walk they have been largely holly, hawthorn or birch, used independently, which co-incidentally makes for easy study. The hawthorn and birch in particular require regular maintenace by laying and cut-*

53

ting to keep it strong and stockproof.

Stanger Spa dates from the 1820s, and was held in the same high regard as the waters at Cheltenham in Gloucestershire. During the summer seasons, the spa was much-frequented by invalids from the surrounding districts. The water contains a high impregnation of marine salt, and was recommended for the treatment of skin and digestive tract disorders: a Sunday afternoon stroll to Stanger Spa was a regular outing for the people of Cockermouth.

The stone building was erected over the well to provide shelter and seating, and the well itself was lined with dressed stone, with niches in the walls for drinking vessels.

Bottles of Stanger Water, costing sixpence (6d), were des-patched to many parts of the world. Today the waters still flow with vigour, and are free to all who trouble to pass.

Water troughs: After leaving Stanger Spa you pass three water troughs. These are fed by underground streams. The first is near the slate wall shortly after leaving the Spa. To its right stands an iron fence behind which the stream has been uncovered and the ground slopes to allow animal access. Across the field from the wicket gate, a slate wall near a stile marks the location of another trough. The third trough is fed by water from each end, and escaping from the middle. In front of this trough the ground has been cobbled, and on the wall behind is a plaque to the memory of Frances Alexander, and the Diamond Jubilee of Queen Victoria, in June 1897.

WALK 15:
Whitbeck Bridge to Boonbeck

This pleasant walk visits the village of Boonbeck, and the nearby hamlets of High Mill, Scales and Hopebeck. From the grassy track to the fellside farm of High Swinside, there are especially attractive views across pastureland to Darling Fell and Mellbreak.

Start: Layby on B5289, Whitbeck Bridge. GR 156249
Total Distance: 5 km (3 miles)
Height gain: 120 m (395 feet)
Difficulty: Easy: a walk on field paths, farm tracks and quiet country lanes. Fences topped with barbed wire.

THE WALK:

Cross the stile, and follow a beck to a stile on to the road. Turn left to cross the beck. After the bridge take a signposted footpath on your right, running alongside the beck to Highmill Bridge.

Turn left to take the road beside the beck to a junction, and turn right to the next junction at the village of Boonbeck. Go right, over a bridge (on the left is Boonbeck Farm, and to the right a picnic area beside the beck). Follow the road left around the buildings, and ascend the road past the last of the buildings for 100 yards to an iron wicket gate on the right.

Turn right to leave the road on a signposted footpath alongside a fence and haw-thorn hedgerow. At a small iron gate in a wall enter a farmyard and follow the track past the farmhouse. Just as the track turns left, take a signposted stony track on the right, behind a large barn.

Beyond the buildings to your right are the reed-filled remains of a dam. Now, the stony track changes to a pleasant grassy track between low walls and fences, with unkempt hedge-rows.

Stay with the track to High Swinside Farm. Go through a gate and take the track round the top side of the farmhouse to a cattle grid and the farm access track. Follow the track out to the road, turning right to descend to a gate across the road. Keeping with the road, go past a farm called The Hope, and a bridge on a bend, spanning Hope Beck. The road now descends to the

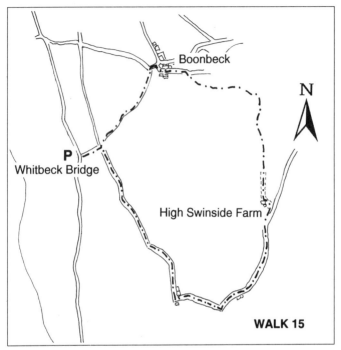

WALK 15

hamlet of Hopebeck. At the road junction turn right, following the road for 2 km (1¼ miles) to a signposted footpath on the left directing you alongside Whit Beck to Whitbeck Bridge.

ALONG THE WAY:
Boonbeck Village *started life as a farming village in the eighteenth-century, has changed significantly over the years, becoming incorporated into the larger village of Lorton. While many of the inhabitants now work in the larger towns of West Cumbria and no longer in farming, the village still maintains a strong community spirit.*

The gate across the road as you descend from High Swinside used to be a common sight on Lakeland roads. Until recently many of the fell roads were unfenced, and gates were used to prevent the sheep from wandering too far. With the increase in motorised traffic the gates became impractical, many were left open, and sheep injured by vehicles. All this has meant fencing the pastures adjoining the roads, and installing cattle grids.

WALK 16:
Mellbreak

Mellbreak is the distinguished whaleback summit along the western flank of Crummock Water. It is one of the so-called Loweswater

Start: Loweswater village, near telephone box. GR 143211. Limited parking
Total Distance: 6 km (4 miles)
Height gain: 460 m (1510 feet)
Difficulty: A tough little summit, involving the ascent of some stretches of scree on which young children will need close supervision. Quite energetic walking.

Fells, a fine twin-topped peak that stands as a sentinel to the Vale of Lorton. The Loweswater Fells are excellent walking country, ranging across fells of modest height and proportion, but no less Lakeland fells for that. They make superb objectives on days when the higher fells elsewhere are thronged.

Like its near neighbour, Hen Comb, Mellbreak stands apart from other summits, without convenient connecting ridges along which to contrive extended walks, and even without dry ground in the valleys across which to fashion a route. Not surprisingly, Mellbreak's shapely form turns the head of many a walker bent on a day on Grasmoor, or the fells of the High Stile range: it is a rough, tough fell, but no one who climbs it is disappointed.

THE WALK:

From the telephone box take the road leading to Loweswater church. There turn left, and then immediately right to gain a road passing Kirkgate Farm (not named on maps). This leads to a gate at the foot of a firebreak through a brief section of forest.

Go up, through the firebreak to reach a broad grassy path heading for the ominous spread of scree and boulders below the northern crags of the fell. There is no need to effect a direct frontal assault on the scree slope, there is a series of zigzags on the left by which the worst of it can be avoided. Higher up, you will soon pick out a notch in the rocks, and when you do, the easiest way is to go straight for it.

This is quite demanding work,

and not a time to lose one's concentration. Young children will need to be watched closely to make sure they don't lose theirs.

Climb through the rocky notch to another zigzagging path that leads to a neat platform, and the opportunity to take a breather.

Taking care to keep children in check, if you take a few steps to your left at this point, around a mini-buttress of rock, you will be rewarded with one of the most outstanding views in Lakeland, reaching out across Crummock Water, Rannerdale and Buttermere to distant Fleetwith Pike at the very head of the dale. Turn about, and the Vale of Lorton is spread at your feet, rising to the lonely outpost of Fellbarrow, and the charming blue-eyed Loweswater itself.

When suitably recovered, continue upwards, on a perfectly obvious route. This will shortly bring you to Mellbreak's first summit, marked by a large cairn, which many people think is the top of the fell. The highest point lies a short distance further on,

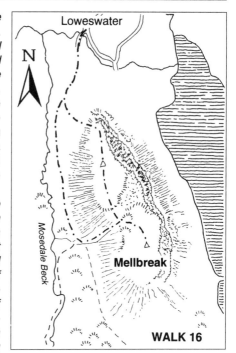

across a damp, broad depression, and is rather less distinguished than the first.

THE WAY BACK:

You can, of course, retrace your steps, but take care descending the scree. Rather easier, is to return to the boggy col, and turn left (west) down steep grassy slopes into Mosedale. In the valley bottom you will find a wet path. Turn right along it to leave the valley northwards. A higher path leads to the top of the firebreak, and so serves the purpose of return equally well.

WALK 17:
Gavel Fell and Blake Fell

These two summits are the highest of the exquisite Loweswater Fells. Their ascent is not unduly difficult, but this walk would rank among the more demanding in this book, and should not be attempted in poor visibility.

Start: Maggie's Bridge car park. GR 135210
Total Distance: 8½ km (5¼ miles)
Height gain: 560 metres (1835 feet)
Difficulty: A fairly energetic walk, mostly on grass. The final descent is very steep, through bilberries and heather.

THE WALK:

Maggie's Bridge car park is a National Trust property, but it is not named on maps. In summer it is a popular spot, so be sure to get there early.

From the car park take a track leading to High Nook Farm, and continue to a gate in the intake wall. Just after the wall, the path forks. Take the left branch, an old drove road leading across the fellside to Whiteoak Beck. When this starts to descend into the Whiteoak valley, leave it for a narrow path, right, climbing around Black Crag. When the path disappears, head for a prominent cairn on the skyline, though this is not the summit of Gavel Fell. By continuing upwards you are forced by fencelines almost on to the summit. A large cairn marks what is commonly accepted as the summit.

To continue to Blake Fell simply follow the fenceline through a series of bends, roughly heading northwards. As you reach the lower slopes of Blake Fell, a couple of stiles enable you to reach a path that leads to a circular shelter, with an impressive view seawards.

THE WAY BACK:

The return to Maggie's Bridge is made by descending Carling Knott, a long arm extending northeast from Blake Fell. The final slope down to rejoin the valley is exceptionally steep, but there is a way of avoiding it.

Retreat to one of two stiles you will have passed as you

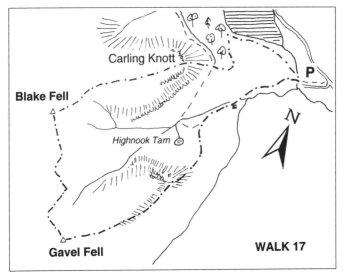

approached the summit of Blake Fell - the fence here is too high for children, and it isn't a good or considerate practice to risk damaging fences by striding over them.

Once across the fence, aim for a series of rocky ledges high above the head of Highnook valley, in which Highnook Tarn gleams brightly. Soon, you reach a minor top, with a rash of cairns, leading downwards to Carling Knott.

Carling Knott is a breathtaking viewpoint, and sufficient reason alone for tackling this walk. The blue of Loweswater, and the spread of Holme Wood seem far, far below, while distance puts a less daunting aspect on Grasmoor's face.

To return to the valley, you set off downwards on an indistinct path through bilberries and heather. This is very steep, and should not be attempted with very young children.

An easier way down can be found simply by going left, northwest and then right, northeast, from the top of Carling Knott, and following a boundary fence until you meet a path, along the boundary of Holme Wood, swinging back beneath the steep slopes of Carling Knott.

Follow the path to Highnook Beck, cross a bridge, and return to the intake gate met with on the ascent. From here it is only a short walk back to Maggie's Bridge car park.

WALK 18:
High Nook Tarn and Holme Beck

This splendid walk on a terraced path above the greenery of Holme Wood, involves only modest expenditure of energy. It is very well suited to summer picnics, and on a clear day has a view across the Solway Firth to Criffel and the Galloway Hills. At quieter times of year, it is a fine walk on which to study birdlife in particular.

Start: Maggie's Bridge car park. GR 135210
Total Distance: 8 km (5 miles)
Height gain: 235m (770 feet)
Difficulty: A fairly easy walk on a broad farm tracks, most grassy. Some wet areas and unbridged streams to cross

THE WALK:

Leave the car park by turning along the road for a short distance to a track on the right. Cross the bridge, and follow a farm track across open fields to High Nook Farm. Go across the farmyard, bearing right in front of the farmhouse to a gate. Climb alongside a wall to a gate, where a grassy track heads clearly across the fellside. Follow this, and when the track descends to a bridge, bear left to ascend to the small, dammed tarn of High Nook.

Retrace your steps to the track, and descend to cross the bridge across Highnook Beck, beyond which a broad track climbs steadily to the edge of Holme Wood, and on to Holme Beck.

Cross the bridge spanning Holme Beck to a grassy terraced track contouring across the fell to a convenient seat, before climbing to a stile. Over the stile, a well-worn track accompanies a wall past two mounds, to a stile and gate from where a grassy track (signposted: Loweswater via Hudson Place) takes you to Iredale Place, and a road.

Turn right to pass Jenkinson Place, where a stone track leads to a stile into a field. Follow a path to a wall opening and hedgerow to the rear of Hudson Place. Waymarking now directs you round the edge of the farm to a road. Turn right (signposted: Holme Wood), and follow the waymarking to the front of the farm, and a stony path leading to

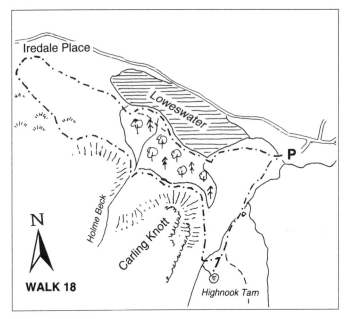

WALK 18

a stone stile into Holme Wood.

A short way into the wood, take a path on the left through broad leaved trees and grassy oases alongside the lake, once again to cross Holme Beck. Head for a stone fishing hut, shortly after which you rejoin the main track, and turn left.

The track now continues for 500 yards to Watergate Farm, where a left turn along the farm access track will take you back to the car park.

ALONG THE WAY:

Holme Wood *was planted between 1945 and 1955 using Sitka and Norway spruce. It stands on the site of an ancient oak woodland. The pines next to the track are Scots pine, and a native British species. During 1994 large areas of spruce were cleared and replanted with sessile oak and larch in an effort to restore the woodland to its former glory.*

Loweswater: *this small lake is tucked away behind Mellbreak, and delightfully set amid woodland. During the summer months the shores are bright with the vivid yellow of marsh marigolds, while in the shallow bays, large lily pads cover the surface with their yellow-white flowers perched decorously on top.*

Other titles by
QUESTA PUBLISHING

WALKS WITH CHILDREN

LAKE DISTRICT
Borrowdale
Buttermere and the Vale of Lorton
Around Coniston
Keswick and the Newlands Valley
Around Ambleside and Grasmere
Ullswater
Around Kendal
Around Windermere
South Lakeland

YORKSHIRE DALES
Wharfedale
Swaledale and Wensleydale

PEAK DISTRICT
Dark Peak

also

SHORT WALKS IN THE EDEN
VALLEY AND NORTH
PENNINES

All QUESTA titles
are available from
PO BOX 520, BAMBER BRIDGE, PRESTON,
LANCASHIRE PR5 8LF

or by FAX to
0870 137 8888
Website: www.questapublishing.co.uk